MW01681429

Secrets of the Invisible Tent

Secrets of the Invisible Tent

Listen, Linger, & Live in God's Presence

SEAN DUNN

BookJourney

Secrets of the Invisible Tent

ISBN (paperback): 978-1-968737-20-7
ISBN (ebook): 978-1-968737-21-4

Library of Congress Control Number: 2026934007

Cover image by Marcin Paśnicki
Interior images from Unsplash
Cover and interior design by Young Design

BookJourney

Published by Book Journey Publishing
Castle Rock, Colorado, USA
Bookjourney.com

Printed in the United States of America

ALSO BY SEAN DUNN

Contending for the Rising Generations: Winning Millennials and Gen Z with the Hope of the Gospel

Contents

Secrets of the Invisible Tent

CLAY BANKS

Introduction

Do you ever find yourself feeling far from God?

Maybe not in what you believe—but in what you *experience*?

Perhaps you want more than routines and familiar words. Perhaps you sense there is a deeper closeness available, a richer life with God, and that longing is what led you to pick up this book.

You know there is more to faith than survival.
You want to experience *all* of God.

It is possible to live your entire Christian life at an unnecessary distance from God.

Not because He is far—but because we are.

That distance can grow quietly and unnoticed. Through fear. Through neglect. Through hidden sin. Through exhaustion. Through disappointment. Through the well-worn habits of religion that teach us how to behave around God but not how to listen to God's voice, to linger in His love, or to live in His presence.

When life with God becomes distant, faith begins to feel fragile—sometimes even irrelevant or dull. The world grows louder. Its opinions grow heavier. Its labels start to stick. And slowly, we forget who we are in Him.

If any of this feels familiar, you are not alone. Many others have felt the same way.

And you are not without hope.

God has always promised His children more than just belief. He promises relationship.

Faith, at its heart, is not about mastering ideas—it is about intimate connection with the living God. And whenever we spend authentic time with Him, something in us changes in ways we could never manufacture on our own.

Although God is everywhere, Scripture is clear that a deeper experience of His nearness is always available to us—a nearness that can be entered intentionally.

And surprisingly, the presence of His nearness can be entered anywhere.

In Scripture, we read that Moses once pitched a simple tent outside the camp—a place where anyone could go to seek the Lord. It was there that God spoke with Moses "face to face, as one speaks to a friend" (Exodus 33:11).

That visual concept became the seed of an idea that has shaped my life.

What if that kind of meeting place was never meant to be confined to the wilderness?

What if God still invites His people into that same closeness today?

This book introduces what I call the "Invisible Tent"—a simple, practical way to remember God's nearness, to enter His presence intentionally, and to cultivate a daily life of listening, healing, and transformation.

In the first part of this book, we will explore Exodus 33:7–11 to uncover the heart and promises behind the original Tent of Meeting. In the second part, we will look at Acts 22:14–15 to discover how this kind of meeting with God shapes our direction, our identity, and our purpose.

This book is your invitation—to learn how to "pitch" a place for God in your everyday life, to linger in His presence, to know His heart, and to live in robust courage that comes from knowing Him personally.

Let me tell you what the invisible tent is not:

The invisible tent is not a formula.

It is not a shortcut.
It is not magic.

The invisible tent is simply a way of remembering what is already true:

God is near.
God is speaking.
God is inviting you closer.

My prayer is that as you learn the secrets of this quiet place, you will discover how to dwell with Him … how to hear Him … how to be strengthened by Him … and how to live in a deeper connection with your Creator than you ever thought possible.

And that once you do …

Your faith will never again be distant.

PART ONE

Pitching the Invisible Tent
Exodus 33:7–11

TOBIAS REICH

— 1 —

The Invitation

I cannot find a word large enough to carry this truth … but I will try.

I am astonished—shocked, awestruck, astounded—that the God of the universe wants a relationship with me.

I am not merely grateful.
I am not merely comforted.
I am *overwhelmed* and *undone* by the fact that the God who spoke light into existence and drove back the darkness, who assigned galaxies their places and calls every star by name, would notice the quiet details of my small life.

That alone is more mercy than I deserve and more wonder than I can fathom. That He bends His attention toward my prayers—desperate, imperfect, sometimes wordless, and often even whiny—is a kindness that *should* leave me amazed.

But even that is not the greatest wonder.

That is only the beginning.

Where I become truly overwhelmed is this: He does not merely listen from a distance.

He invites me close.

The undefeated God.
The uncreated One.
The One with no rival, no equal, no beginning, and no end.

He does not remain a distant majesty, admired from afar but never approached. Instead, He steps toward me. He makes room. He opens His arms and says, *Come closer.*

Come and enjoy My presence.
Come and be surrounded by My nearness.
Come and be filled with My wisdom.
Come and behold My beauty.
Come and learn My heart.
Come and get lost in My grace.

This is the holy and staggering truth of the gospel to me—that the Sovereign of the universe does not merely tolerate my approach but *desires* it. That the One who holds all things together wants to hold my attention. That the God who needs nothing chooses relationship.

As I have journeyed through this life, it is this truth—this invitation—that has continued to astonish me day after day. Entering into His presence has become a holy addiction of my soul.

After decades of enjoying the intimate relationship He offers, I stand here amazed again—aware that even now my words are too small—that the mightiest and most powerful force ever to exist is also tender and personal, and that His attention and affection are fixed on me as though I were the only one.

Even though I am small, self-absorbed, and unremarkable …

How can this be true?

How can the Holy and All-Powerful One want me to come close?

FROM WONDER TO WELCOME

When I speak about God's desire to be close, I am not speaking in abstracts.

I am speaking about an invitation.

Not a metaphorical one.
Not a poetic idea.
But a real, deliberate, personal invitation from God Himself.

Every invitation carries certain elements: a host, a guest list, a purpose, a place, a time, and something to bring.

This one has all of them.

The **host** is God … and He is waiting … intentionally.
The **guest list** includes you and me … the only question is, will we go?
The **purpose** is simple and staggering … to meet with Him and to be changed by His presence and what He reveals.
The **place** is wherever you are … all that is required is a hungry heart and undivided attention.
The **time** is now … He is available whenever you are willing to come.
And **what must you bring**? Nothing but your attention and a willing heart.

This is not an invitation merely to learn about God, but to know Him. Not to study Him at a distance, but to walk with Him in the ordinary rhythms of life—to bring Him into every challenge, every dream, every loss, every hope, every ordinary (or unusual) moment in between.

Many people know *about* God without ever truly knowing Him.

Some have encountered Him once or twice but long for more.
Some believe yet feel unsure of how to hear His voice.
Some wonder what He desires for them, or whether He is near at all.
And some—perhaps you—have quietly concluded that God is real but distant … holy but removed … powerful but strangely uninvolved.

I once felt that way too.

Until I accepted this invitation.

And it changed everything.

What still leaves me stunned is not only that our Creator rules the universe, but that He desires to be known by His creation, that He does not simply observe our lives but invites us into His presence to hear His voice and learn His heart.

This invitation is not new.

It is ancient.

But it is still relevant today!

INSPIRED BY AN ACTUAL TENT

To help you discover the beauty of this invitation, I want to offer you a gift.

A gift that I have come to affectionately call the Invisible Tent.

Before I explain the gift I'm about to place in your hands, we need to visit a different tent.

Not an invisible one. A real one.

The idea came about because God so valued connection and communication with Moses (and others). Scripture tells us in Exodus 33:7–11 that during the Israelites' journey through the wilderness, Moses would set up a tent outside the camp—a portable, temporary tabernacle—where he met with God:

> *Now Moses used to take a tent and pitch it outside the camp some distance away, calling it the "tent of meeting." Anyone inquiring of the LORD would go to the tent of meeting outside the camp. And whenever Moses went out to the tent, all the people rose and stood at the entrance to their tents, watching Moses until he entered the tent. As Moses went into the tent, the pillar of cloud would come down and stay at the entrance, while the LORD spoke with Moses. Whenever the people saw the pillar of cloud standing at the entrance to the tent, they all stood and worshiped, each at the entrance to their tent. The LORD would speak to Moses face to face, as one speaks to a friend. Then Moses would return to the camp, but his young aide Joshua son of Nun did not leave the tent.*

MATTHEW SMITH

God is near, and
I can meet with Him
right now.

I love that phrase—*face-to-face, as one speaks to a friend.* It reveals the authentic connection and relationship that the two enjoyed.

Not thunder and lightning … although there was a cloud.

Not distant commands shouted from heaven.

But friendship.

Conversation.

Nearness.

As well as direction.

Inspiration.

And counsel.

This tent was not a religious performance stage. It was not a temple with crowds and ceremony. It was a simple, portable space where an ordinary man met with an extraordinary God.

That's the pattern.

A movable meeting place.

An intentional withdrawal from noise.
A sacred space for real relationship.

Now, here's where things get a little unconventional.
I do not travel with a canvas tent.
I don't carry tent poles in my trunk.

And yet, for years, I have been handing out tents to people everywhere I go.

Thousands of them.
Maybe hundreds of thousands by now.
Invisible ones.

And remarkably, they fit every pocket, every schedule, every personality, and every season of life.

No assembly required. No instructions in twelve confusing languages. No missing pieces.

Just a simple way to remember:

God is near, and I can meet with Him right now.

That is the gift I want to give you.

If you take it and learn to use it, it will change your life—ongoing and forever.

THE INVISIBLE VISUAL AID

In front of you is quite possibly the most interesting gift you will ever receive. It is a little bit strange. It was contrived in the imagination of a former youth pastor, after all. But it is a very meaningful and highly effective gift. It may just be the gift you never knew you needed.

This gift is the tool at the heart of this book. I will show you how to open it, and then spend the rest of these pages teaching you how to use this gift as it was intended.

The gift is a tent.

Here—take it. This one is yours.

Can you see it in your mind's eye?

It will be invisible to others … but not to you.

Your tent is uniquely yours.

It isn't mass-produced.
You define its qualities.
You choose its features.

What color is it?
Red? Forest green? Sky blue?
What shape is it?
Can you see the flap where you enter?
Does it have a playlist?
Rooms?

Perhaps a room that reminds you to pray for your family and friends, with pictures hanging on invisible walls.

Your tent may change over time.

That's okay.

You don't have to design every detail right now. That will come as you continue to use it. All that matters is that you understand what it represents—and what awaits inside.

The tent itself is imaginary.
But its impact is very real.

Because God is waiting to meet you in a personal and profound way every time you step inside.

And because it is imaginary, it is always with you.

You'll never leave it at home.

Because it is invisible, you can always find room to use it.

At a stoplight.
In a prayer meeting in church.
In a break room at work.
In a busy airport.
In your bed at night.

Some locations scream "spiritual," but even the ones that don't become holy as you pull out your tent to meet with Him.

> *Your invisible tent brings instant focus that promises real connection with God.*

There is one crucial characteristic of your tent you should know up front. You can have confidence because your tent is spiked on solid ground, the promise of God's presence.

Yet it is movable—you can take it with you and pitch it anywhere. He will always meet you whenever you open it up.

Now, I realize this gift may feel unusual. After all, who uses something invisible as a visual aid?

Still, this image has been deeply meaningful to me and to many others.

I've given away countless invisible tents and some of

the responses have been entertaining.

People have asked to take pictures with them and their tents.

I've received emails saying, "I showed my tent to my spouse … they don't get it."

Others tell me they use theirs every day, in all kinds of places. "I never leave home without it."

I had one young lady run up to me in an airport, thanking me for the tent I gave her at her college a couple of years before.

I had a pastor invite me to his church because he loved his tent and wanted me to give everyone in his church one.

This is interesting to me because the tent isn't real …

Or is it? The tent is real in the ways that matter.

The invisible tent might not be literal canvas, but it does literally set the tone for me and many others to connect with God intimately.

Hopefully, it will for you too.

And even if it doesn't …

My prayer is that you will embrace its principles—
And accept God's invitation to go deeper with Him.

WHERE HE HAS MET ME

I am not writing about this tent as a theory.

I am writing about it as a man who has been built as well as held together by God because of it.

He has revealed vision. He has spoken encouragement, and He has communicated promises. But there were also times when He surrounded me with His indescribable love and grace when I was in deep and dark struggles.

Several years ago, my life cracked open in ways I never saw coming. The kind of season that disorients you. The kind that makes you question not only your future but yourself. I carried grief, confusion, disappointment, and a quiet fear that something essential in me had been lost for good.

And so, I drove.

In an old beat-up car with more miles than dignity, I drove through my neighborhood … then farther … then into the mountains near my home in Castle Rock, Colorado. I talked to God out loud. I sat in silence. I asked questions I never received answers to. I released others I eventually learned I didn't need answered.

And somewhere between the steering wheel and the silence, I pitched my tent.

I did not escape the pain. But I was not alone in it.

In that invisible meeting space, God did not lecture me. He did not hurry me. He did not minimize what

I was carrying. He met me there—with a peace that made no sense, a steadiness I could not manufacture, and a quiet assurance that I was still His.

Scripture calls it "a peace that transcends all understanding" (Philippians 4:7). I can only tell you that it guarded me when nothing else could.

One afternoon during that season, a wise older woman from our church stopped by my office. She said simply, "Sean, I was praying this morning, and I believe God wants to speak to you today. Take your Bible. Go to the sanctuary. Listen."

So, I did.

I sat alone on the steps of a converted warehouse sanctuary, staring at worn green carpet, and I pitched my tent again.

After a long silence, my eyes fell on Isaiah 61:7:

> *"Instead of your shame you will receive a double*

portion … and everlasting joy will be yours."

Those words had been written centuries earlier, but they landed in me like a personal letter.

Not in an audible voice—but with unmistakable clarity. I sensed God say:

I have not forgotten you.
You are not finished.
You are not broken beyond repair.
I will rebuild what has been shaken.

In that tent, God did more than comfort me.

He re-anchored my identity.
He steadied my calling.
He reminded me who I was when everything else felt uncertain.

And slowly, faithfully, He began to rebuild my life from the inside out.

That is why I believe this invitation is real.

That is why I believe God still meets people.

That is why I believe tents still work.

Christ has never failed me—only forgiven me. He has never forgotten me—only waited for me. He has never withdrawn His presence—only invited me back into it.

And that promise is not unique to me. I have seen it work for countless others.

It is also offered to you.

Whenever you turn your attention toward Him, He is already there. Whenever you step into His presence, something in you begins to heal, align, and awaken.

That is what the invisible tent is for.

And that is your invitation now:

To learn how to meet Him.
To listen.
To be restored.
And to walk back into your life carrying more of God than you did before.

The host is waiting.

The tent is ready.

Will you go?

— 2 —

Anyone Can Go In

When Moses pitched his tent in the wilderness, something simple and holy began to unfold. He was stepping into God's presence—not as a ritual but as a relationship made possible by God's personal nature.

Moses wasn't putting on a show.
He wasn't performing religion.
He was entering with quiet confidence that God would meet him there.

In those few verses of Exodus 33, we are not given a theory of prayer or a system of worship.

Instead …

We are given a picture.

A real-life glimpse of what happens when a human life makes room for a holy God.

And within that picture are four quiet principles that are unchanging, generous, and still available to us today.

These principles form the simple framework of the Tent of Meeting:

1. Anyone can go in.
2. God's presence will show up.
3. Intimate communication will take place.
4. And you can stay as long as you want.

These four truths will guide our life in the tent.

But before we learn how to pitch our own …

We must first watch Moses step into his.

PETER THOMAS

How many today
never take the
steps to know God
personally?

THE WALK

When I picture Moses and the Israelites camped in the desert, I imagine a wide community of black and tan woven tents scattered in wandering rows with a long open aisle running through the middle. It may not be perfectly accurate, but in my mind I see Moses advancing through the corridor of tents—staff in hand, face set with purpose—making his way toward the tent he had pitched outside the camp.

Even though Joshua, his young assistant, would sometimes join him, this wasn't a social activity.

That tent had only one purpose:

To meet with God.

Scripture tells us that whenever Moses began that walk, the people would emerge from their tents. I picture fathers gathering their families. Mothers pausing their work. Children trailing behind, curious and wide-eyed, because Moses—the man who spoke with God—was passing through.

Everyone stood at the entrances of their tents and watched.

When the pillar of cloud visited the entrance to the tent while Moses remained inside (we will get into that in the next chapter), the people worshipped from where they were.

They stood. They watched. They worshipped from a distance as their leader took his turn with God inside the Tent of Meeting.

And I've often wondered: How many of the Israelites—who were also invited to meet with God inside the Tent of Meeting—never took their turn?

The invitation was open. The promise was that "*anyone* inquiring of the Lord" could go to the tent.

Anyone.

Yet I imagine many stayed where they were.

Close enough to observe.
Close enough to be inspired.
Close enough to worship.

But not motivated enough to enter.

Perhaps they told themselves, *Moses hears God for us.*
Perhaps they thought, *That kind of closeness is for leaders … for prophets … for people holier than me.*
Perhaps they were afraid. Or distracted. Or simply comfortable standing at a distance.

They believed in God.

They desired to honor God.

They worshipped God.

But they never stepped into the place where God was waiting to speak to them personally.

NOTHING HAS CHANGED ...

The reason I ask the question—*How many of them never entered the tent?*—is because I wonder the same about people today.

How many today never take the steps to know God personally?

How many are content knowing that their pastors hear His voice ... that their leaders receive His peace ... that others experience His guidance and encouragement—while they themselves remain at a distance?

They believe.
They admire.
They attend church.
They worship.
They may even serve.

But they never enter God's presence inside the tent.

The promises of the invisible tent are for every believer. Yet many will never fully experience God's presence, never learn to recognize His voice, never begin to grasp the depth of His personal and relentless love.

Not because the invitation is unclear, but because life feels louder or priorities are misaligned.

Distractions multiply.
Busyness dominates.
Comfort lulls the spirit to sleep.

And slowly, the doorway to the tent becomes ordinary … and unentered.

Even though most indicate that they want to be close to God, the lack of intentionality proves that noble idea is not a goal, just a wish.

However, anyone who chooses to build a habit of entering the tent will discover something altogether unexpected—but profoundly meaningful.

They will hear God's gentle affirmations.
They will receive clarity and vision for their lives.

They will be strengthened with courage.
They will gain access to His wisdom.
They will learn to love more deeply and live more freely.

Yet, entering the tent to be with God will cost something.

You must walk past the distractions.
You must resist the tyranny of what feels urgent.
You must say no to what merely entertains but never transforms.

It takes discipline.
It takes resolve.
It takes spiritual priority.

And it takes rhythm.

The tent was never meant to be visited occasionally—it was meant to be entered regularly. The more time you spend in God's presence, the more deeply His transforming work takes root in your life.

If you never enter, the benefits remain distant stories.

But inside the tent …

The secrets are revealed.

And they come alive.

— 3 —

God's Presence Will Show Up

The tent is not about practicing stale religion or phoning in spiritual duty. It is not about checking boxes or perfecting routines.

It is about connection.

It is about drawing near to the Creator of the universe.

It is about quieting the noise and chaos of the world and turning your full attention and affection toward Jesus—the One who paid the price so that we could know God intimately.

Scripture gives us a beautiful and daring promise:

> *When we draw near to Him, He will draw near to us.*

This is articulated in the New Testament in James 4:8 and is evidenced all through Scripture and all throughout history. God is available and approachable. He does not hide behind the proverbial curtain. He is not distant to those who long to know Him.

When we set aside distractions and make Him our priority, He does not stay back and observe us in our striving. He comes close.

This promise is the foundation of life in the tent.

Closeness is not built on our effort and energy alone—although spiritual discipline is important. Connection is the reward of a Good Father who wants to be close to His child. And intimacy is sustained by God's faithful response to every sincere step we take toward Him.

LAURINE BAILLY

Intimacy is sustained by God's faithful response to every sincere step we take toward Him.

MOSES AND THE PROMISE IN ACTION

This deep fellowship is exactly what Moses experienced.

Scripture tells us that whenever Moses entered the tent, a pillar of cloud—the visible expression of God's presence—would descend and remain at its entrance.

Moses was not left waiting and wondering.
He was not left hoping for attention.
He was not left speaking into silence.

Each time he entered the tent, Moses encountered the living presence of the all-powerful and conversational God. (We will examine that in the next chapter.)

God did not leave Moses alone.

God met him there.

IT WORKED FOR KELLY

Kelly came to church every week.

She had for most of her life.

She knew the songs. She knew when to stand and when to bow her head. She believed in God. She loved Him. She was grateful for salvation and forgiveness.

But she was exhausted.

Kelly carried a constant weight of anxiety and quiet depression. She rarely felt like she was enough—never enough as a mother, never enough as a wife, never enough as a person, never enough as a Christian. Her days were loud and demanding, full of responsibility yet empty of rest.

She loved her child deeply, but motherhood had overwhelmed her. The chaos—the lack of sleep, the endless demands, the loss of silence—felt heavier than she had ever expected. There was no space to breathe. No space to think. No space to be still.

Her faith was no practical help.

She prayed, but mostly to make it through the day.
She asked for help, but never for closeness.
She went to church, but not to meet with God.

Her relationship with Him had slowly become about rules, structure, and doing the right thing—habits formed in childhood that never quite matured into relationship.

She just didn't know there was another way to live.

She didn't know that God was eagerly waiting for permission to invade her life and meet her needs.

One Sunday I was invited to speak at the church we both attend. I shared about the Tent of Meeting—about God's invitation, His nearness, and the simple but profound practice of intentionally entering His presence. I shared how God waits, how He draws near, how peace is something that is promised and found in His company.

And I offered what I always do.

An invisible tent. A simple way to remember that God is near and available—anytime, anywhere.

Kelly listened.

Something stirred.

She decided she would accept the gift of an invisible visual aid and she would try.

Over the next several weeks, she began to "pitch her tent."

Sometimes it was in the stillness while her child slept.
Sometimes it was in the car on the way to a doctor's appointment.

Sometimes it was in silence.
Sometimes it was in the middle of the noise of her ordinary life.

I am sure it felt foreign and strange, but she didn't give up.

And slowly, something changed.

She began to sense God's presence—her heart started to find rest. She was feeling less overwhelmed. The constant edge of fear softened. The heaviness that followed her around the house began to loosen its grip.

Peace didn't arrive all at once.

It grew.

Two months later, she pulled my wife aside after church.

With gratitude in her heart, she explained how her spiritual life had changed since she moved from religious routine into intentional time alone with God.

Her relationship with Jesus had become personal.
Her thoughts had become steadier.
Her emotions less overwhelming.
Her life—still full, still demanding—had become manageable.

Hope had returned.

Not because her challenging circumstances disappeared. But because she was no longer facing them alone.

Kelly didn't find a new religion. She didn't need a new God.

She needed a meeting place.

She needed to know how to meet with God and invite His comforting and guiding presence.

She discovered the mystery of the tent. She started to use it, and God met her there.

THE SAME PROMISE FOR YOU

The first two principles of the Tent of Meeting are simple and life-changing:

Anyone can go in.
God's presence will show up.

I am not promising that a cloud will fill your room every time you set aside time for God as it did with Moses.

But I am reaffirming something far better:

> *God has promised to draw near to you when you choose to draw near to Him.*

And when He does, every part of His nature comes with Him.

He is the God of peace … and He will quiet your heart.
He is a healing God … and He will tend to your wounds with care.
He is a wise God … and He will guide your uncertain steps.
He is a loving God … and He will remind you that you are cared for.
He is a restoring God … and He will rebuild parts of your life that have been fractured.

When you spend time in the tent, your faith becomes more than doctrine and duty—it becomes experience … because you are met by the Faithful One.

Your courage grows … because you hear from the Undefeated One.

Your anxiety loosens its grip … because your attention shifts to the Giver of Hope, the Protector, and the One who holds your future.

And slowly, quietly, beautifully, something deeper happens.
You realize you are no longer seeking His gifts.
You are enjoying *Him*.

You start to find yourself satisfied—not in what He gives …

But in who He is.

— 4 —

Intimate Communication Will Take Place

"I always thought God was distant."
"I always thought He was angry with me."
"I never felt good enough."
"I had no idea He wanted me to approach Him as a friend."

I have heard some version of these words more times than I can count.

For many people, an angry or impersonal God was modeled for them—not a loving, compassionate, and kind Father. Not a God who draws near. Not a God who delights in relationship.

This perception of a distant, dissatisfied God is common.

But it is not accurate.

Scripture paints a very different picture.
The Bible is clear: God is deeply relational.
James tells us that Abraham was called "God's friend" (James 2:23).

King David, overwhelmed by God's attention, wrote:

> *"What is mankind that you are mindful of them, human beings that you care for them?" (Psalm 8:4).*

And Jesus Himself said:

> *"I no longer call you servants … I have called you friends" (John 15:15).*

And Moses experienced this kind of closeness. Scripture tells us that:

> *"The Lord would speak to Moses face to face, as one speaks to a friend" (Exodus 33:11).*

MAAJA WEBER

Can you imagine that?

Friendship with an indescribable God.

MOSES AND GOD

Can you imagine that?

Friendship with the indescribable God.

Moses did not lower his voice into a religious tone.
He did not perform.
He did not pretend.

He spoke honestly.

Face-to-face.
Heart-to-heart.

Without pretense.
Without shame.
Without fear of rejection.
Without being bound by insecurity.

And God met him there in the same way.

With compassion.
With truth.

With direction.
With correction when needed.
And—if I may imagine—with warmth and even laughter.

As friends.

Let that settle for a moment.

A CONVERSATION, NOT A MONOLOGUE

A few years ago, I was meeting with a friend who also happens to be a counselor. In the middle of our conversation, he paused, looked at me, and said something that caught me off guard.

"Sean, you're an extrovert. Do you know what that means?"

I smiled. "Of course. It means I like to talk."

He laughed, shook his head, and said, "No. It means you *need* to talk. You don't always know what you think until you hear yourself say it out loud."

That diagnosis stayed with me.

Because he was right.

I don't process in silence. My thoughts don't line up neatly on their own. I need to speak them. I need to wrestle with ideas out loud. I need to explore possibilities, name concerns, test decisions, and sort through emotions in conversation.

Whether it's strategy for business, challenges with our adult children, doors that might be opening, or questions about what God is teaching me, I almost always reach for someone I trust—my wife, Jené; a coworker; a board member; or a close friend.

As I talk, clarity comes.

And over time, I realized something important about myself: I am wired the same way with God.

I need to talk to Him every day—not just about outcomes, not just with a list of requests, but honestly and vulnerably.

I've learned that He welcomes my thoughts, my fears, my hopes, my questions, and my plans. He invites me to name my insecurities, confess my weaknesses, and speak openly about the wounds I carry.

God is an amazing listener.

And there is something healing about hearing my voice while speaking to my God. It confirms that I am fully known and still fully loved.

But I've also learned this:

He doesn't want our relationship to be one-sided.

Healthy friendships are never monologues. One person should never dominate the conversation. There should be dialogue and exchange.

Yet we often treat God as if He is there to take in but never to impart.

We speak.
We unload.
We present our agenda.

And then we leave.

The tent is not meant to be a place we offer a report or a wish list. We are not sitting on Santa's lap to confirm our requests or phoning in a pizza order with our demands.

The invisible tent is a meeting place.

A place for dialogue.
A place to speak—and to listen.
A place where the God who sees everything shares His heart, His wisdom, and His perspective with those who are willing to linger long enough to hear Him.

THE SAME GOD, THE SAME INVITATION

This is one of the great truths of the tent:

Inside it, you encounter a presence you did not expect . . .
A relationship deeper than you imagined . . .
A connection more personal than you were taught to believe possible.

As I write this, I'm reminded of an old Looney Tunes cartoon. Hugo the Abominable Snowman is a huge, awkward character who desperately wants companionship. Pleading for attention and a friend, he keeps pursuing Bugs Bunny, declaring, "I will hug him and squeeze him, and I will call him George."

In some ways, that cartoon feels like humanity.

Awkward.
Clumsy.
Longing to be noticed.
Craving affection.
Desperate to be known.

You would think *we* would be the ones chasing God.

But here is the surprise:

He is the One pursuing us.
He is the One waiting for us to look up.
He is the One calling our name.
He is the One inviting friendship.

Not because He lacks something.

But because He loves.

He wants to bless us and encourage us—not only with His presence but with His friendship.

He wants us to feel seen.
He wants us to feel heard.
He wants us to know we are not alone.
He wants to steady us when we are afraid.
He wants to speak truth when we are confused.
He wants to celebrate our victories.
And He wants to sit with us in our pain.

In the tent, faith moves from transaction to relationship.
From duty to delight.
From distance to friendship.

God still speaks to His people the way a friend speaks to a friend.

Not because He needs it.

But because He wants it.

And we receive the breathtaking gift of being loved personally by a perfect God.

– 5 –

You Can Stay as Long as You Want

There were times when Joshua, Moses's apprentice, would join him in the tent, and I find it fascinating that the account in Exodus makes a point to tell us that when Moses left the tent, Joshua stayed behind.

That detail speaks volumes to me.

Joshua was a young man standing on the edge of his leadership destiny—busy learning from Moses, carrying responsibility, wrestling with uncertainty, and trying to understand his calling. Yet, he was so captivated by God's presence that His holy presence became Joshua's priority.

He didn't just fulfill a requirement.
He didn't opt for the minimum.
He lingered.

He was so captivated—so caught up in God's nearness—that he didn't want the moment to end.

And I believe this is what begins to happen as we practice meeting with God in the tent.

Spending time with God stops feeling like labor.
It stops feeling like duty.

Opportunity replaces the obligation.

A holy addiction begins to grow.

After all,
Who willingly walks away from a relationship that brings peace to the core of the soul?
Who ends a conversation that is filled with clarity and encouragement?
Who cuts time short with the One who created them, loves them, guides them, and strengthens their purpose?

When we understand the beauty and benefit of being

with God, we begin earlier, stay longer, and build our days around Him.

FROM DISCIPLINE TO DESIRE

In all honesty, I did not always live this way.

Even as a young pastor, I prayed out of obligation and read Scripture only as preparation. God was part of my work, not yet the center of my affection.

I rushed my "quiet time."
I did my duty.
I checked the box.
I gave Him leftovers.

I never stayed long enough to be changed.

That wasn't my goal.

To be transparent, I wanted to be a strong communicator. I wanted to represent myself well as a pastor. In my pursuit of excellence in my pastoral role, I was not yet longing for His presence. And I was not dedicated to this discipline.

Then something shifted.

I don't remember exactly why—perhaps someone challenged me—but I began to carve out time. I made Him my focus. I made listening and resting my goal.

I stopped rushing.

Instead of racing through requests, I thanked Him for His nearness. I slowed my heart. I took deep breaths. I set distractions aside. I learned to be still.

That was the beginning of real transformation.

In His presence, I sensed Him carrying my burdens.
His peace settled over me.
Joy replaced heaviness.
Encouragement touched my deepest insecurities.

In His nearness, I felt seen, heard, known, and loved.

And the more time I spent with Him, the more I craved.

Eventually, my "quiet time" stopped being something I *had* to do.

It became something I *couldn't wait* to do.

I wasn't there to prepare sermons.
Or to grow intellectually.
Or to perform spiritually.

I was there to be with my favorite Friend.

ADDICTED TO HIS PRESENCE

For more than forty years, I have lived in vocational ministry with two driving passions.

First, I am an evangelist. I wake up thinking about people who do not know Jesus—about how to reach the broken, the searching, and the forgotten. Those who need Him but will not seek Him on their own.

Second, I want people to know how personal God is. I want them to know that every minute spent with Him is so much better than every minute apart.

This is not just something I preach. It is something that flows over and out of my life.

Solitude with Jesus has changed me—and it continues to change me.

I want others to discover what I have discovered: God meets every need, answers the deepest questions, and pours out His goodness on those who accept His invitation to closeness. I want them to know that His greatest rewards are set aside for those who regularly seek Him (Hebrews 11:6) and prioritize time with Him.

Those who understand this begin to sound like Joshua:

I want more.
I don't want to leave.

BERTRAND BORIE

In His nearness, I felt seen, heard, known, and loved.

WHEN PEOPLE "GET IT"

I once had dinner with a group of college students. The conversation turned to a popular TV show everyone was watching. Everyone talked excitedly—except one young woman named Mindy.

When someone asked her if she had seen it, she said quietly:

> *"I was watching with my family ... but when the show started, I sensed God inviting me to come close. So, I went to my room and opened my Bible."*

She felt God invite her into the tent to spend time with Him and nothing was more important to her.

Another man I know went even further.

He sold his television.

Not out of legalism—but because he wanted fewer distractions and more time with God.

For me, it means guarding my mornings. I've learned that I meet God best early—before the noise and demands of the day claim my attention. Flights, meetings, schedules—those come later.

God comes first.

And I want to say this plainly:

> *When you discover the beauty of being with Him, you will want more.*

Time alone with God will become your priority.

And if you let it …

It will become your addiction.

Not all addictions destroy.

Some rebuild.
Some heal.
Some restore.

When time with God becomes your deepest craving, your life grows stronger, steadier, and fuller—and the fruit becomes visible to you as well as to everyone around you.

The invitation still stands.

I offer you an invisible tent.

But God offers you something greater:

> *A relationship marked by intimacy, closeness, and ongoing conversation.*

Remember:

> *Anyone can go in.*
> *God's presence will meet you there.*
> *Intimate communication will follow.*
> *And you can stay as long as you want.*

And if you are still reading, something in you already longs for this kind of connection.

So, let's continue.

What happens in the tent?
How do we listen?
How do we draw near?
How does God change us there?

Keep going.

It only gets better from here.

PART TWO

From Lingering to Leaving

Acts 22:14–15

– 6 –

Chosen for a Purpose

If I were to ask you, "What did God choose you for?" how would you answer?

Would you say He chose you to be a preacher?
A business leader?
A disciple-maker?
A servant to the poor?

A writer, teacher, accountant, or athlete?

Will your impact be felt most by your family … your community … or the nations?

All of those roles, responsibilities, and passions are meaningful, and they may be things you pursue. But there is more. Before God commissions you to go anywhere, achieve anything, or accomplish any task, the first and most important calling on your life is that you know Him.

HE WAS CHOSEN

In Acts 22, Scripture records the dramatic conversion of Saul of Tarsus—later known as Paul the Apostle.

He would become one of the greatest influences in the early church and the most prolific missionary our faith has ever known.

But at this point in the story, Saul was far from a follower of Jesus.

He had completely misunderstood who God was and what God was doing.

He was not advancing the gospel.

He was trying to destroy it.

He hunted believers.

He approved of Stephen's execution.
He was consumed with religious commitment and violent devotion.

Saul was on a mission—a mission he believed God had given him—to arrest and silence anyone who followed Jesus.

And it was at the height of that misguided passion that God intervened.

Jesus—the very One Saul wanted erased—appeared to him on the road to Damascus.

A light from heaven surrounded Saul.
He fell to the ground.

And Jesus spoke:

> *"I am Jesus of Nazareth, whom you are persecuting."*

Saul was told to enter the city and wait for further instructions.

Blind and shaken, he was led by his companions into Damascus.

Days later, God sent a man named Ananias to pray for Saul. When Ananias prayed, something like scales fell from Saul's eyes, and his sight was restored.

But the miracle was not finished.

The most important moment was still coming.

We read in Acts that Ananias looked at Saul and said:

> *"The God of our ancestors has chosen you to know His will, to see the Righteous One, and to hear words from His mouth. You will be His witness to all people of what you have seen and heard" (Acts 22:14–15).*

I imagine Ananias pausing after that first sentence.

"God has chosen you."

Yes, Saul would travel the world.

Yes, he would plant churches.
Yes, he would write Scripture.
Yes, he would leave an astonishing legacy.

But that was not the first thing God said about him.

God did not begin with assignment.

He began with relationship.

To paraphrase Ananias:

> *God has chosen you to know Him.*

Everything else flowed from that.

And the same is true for you.

You may write.
You may preach.
You may lead.
You may build.

You may accomplish more than you can currently imagine.

But God's first calling on your life is not your ministry, calling, or mission.

It is your relationship.

You have been chosen to know your Creator deeply, intimately, and personally.

Because when you do …

You discover wisdom for every decision.
Strength for every season.
Peace for every storm.
Purpose for every step.

You don't just do great things.

You do the things He created you to do.

And you do them with Him.

As you get to know Him, you discover the abundant life that Scripture promises, the eternal purpose that you were created for, and the impact that you crave.

WHERE IT BEGINS

According to Acts 22:14, God's invitation to Paul unfolded in this order:

You are chosen to:

Know His will
See the Righteous One
Hear words from His mouth

Then …

You become a witness of what you have seen and heard.

Then …

He defines and empowers your mission.

Then …

He entrusts you with impact.

Thousands of years ago, Saul of Tarsus set out on a mission. He thought he knew how to serve God.

But one encounter with Jesus—and one conversation with Ananias—changed everything.

His ambition changed.
His direction changed.
Even his identity changed … as evidenced by eventually choosing to use his Greek name, Paul, so he could better fulfill his mission to the non-Jews.

His goal was no longer religion.

It was relationship.

And when we realize that we, too, have been chosen to know Him, the same transformation begins in us.

DANIELA KOKINA

The God of our fathers has chosen you to know Him!

Who we are changes.
What we pursue changes.
Why and how we live changes.

So, let's step through the open door of the tent.

Let's learn how to know God—not as a concept, not as a duty, but as a friend.

Because you were not just chosen to serve Him.

You were chosen for a bigger purpose.

The God of our fathers has chosen you to know Him!

– 7 –

To Know His Will

The God of the universe wants you and me to know His will.

How crazy is that?

Not only does He promise to listen to our prayers—which in itself is beyond comprehension—but the God of all creation wants to share His thoughts with us.

He wants us to perceive what He is thinking, planning, and orchestrating on our behalf. He even reveals truths about what we are seeing in the crazy world around us.

And when we pitch our tent, crawl in, quiet ourselves, shut out distractions, and focus on Him, He begins to whisper.

So, let's dig into that and figure out how to best posture ourselves to hear His voice.

BLOCKING OUT OTHER VOICES

When we turn our attention to Him, we are pitching the invisible tent—and He is ready.

Whenever we draw near to Him, He draws near to us. That is His promise. He is always waiting for us to slow down so He can engage and encourage.

Whether we meet Him in the morning in our favorite chair or take advantage of a few quiet minutes in a coffee shop before friends arrive, He will invade our space and speak with us.

He is just waiting for us to shut out the noise and invite Him close.

We live with confidence, not only that His blessings are ours, but that the presence He promises is always available. When we look up, He is near and ready to speak.

So, breathe deeply, release the stress that pulls at your attention, and receive the peace He offers.

Do not start by talking but by resting—as this is a great practice. Enjoy being near Him. Sit and abide.

The longer we sit, aware of His presence, the closer we feel to Him—and the further we feel from everyday struggles.

These moments of quiet connection are worth the price of admission. They are like a massage for the soul, releasing tension and easing the weight of life. Eventually, though, we turn to Him and invite Him to speak.

"God, what is on Your heart today?
What do You want to say?
What do You want me to know?
What do You want me to do?"

Then we take our proverbial notepad and begin to listen … jotting mental notes as we go.

He may speak about the child who keeps you up at night, or the parent you are struggling with.
He may add names to your prayer list—family members with health issues or hearts He longs to draw closer to.
He may speak about your business, or prompt you to call a friend you haven't spoken to in years.

When you prioritize tent time with the Lord and invite Him to share His will, you allow Him to lead the conversation, trusting that His perfect perspective will shape it.

Before we go further, let me say it again:

God wants you to know His will.
He is not hiding. He is not withholding.
He is eager to guide and direct you.

The question is … are we ready to listen?

A RENEWED MIND

The apostle Paul explained to the Christians in Rome that transformation must come before clarity. When our mind operates in worldly patterns, our ability to discern God's will is limited.

To truly recognize His direction, we must be transformed by the renewing of our mind.

> *Do not conform to the pattern of this world, but be transformed by the renewing of your mind. Then you will be able to test and approve what God's will is—His good, pleasing, and perfect will (Romans 12:2).*

Our mind thinks about self-protection and focuses on selfish things, but that is not how God thinks. He is playing 3D chess, while our minds are playing checkers. He is thinking about everyone and everything all at once, while we are limited to what impacts us.

We think immediate. He thinks eternal.
We think comfort. He thinks character.
We think wants. He thinks needs.

We think blessings and addition. He thinks impact and multiplication.

So, if we want to know His "good, pleasing, and perfect will," we must invite Him to reshape how we think.

Not only our actions—but our perspective.

Some ask, "How?"

A transformed mind is not a destination but a journey—and one worth pursuing.

The journey toward a transformed mind takes discipline—spiritual and mental.

Spiritual disciplines (Scripture reading, prayer, worship, rhythms of rest) shape our thinking.

Mental discipline means taking our thoughts captive (2 Corinthians 10:5) and not letting inappropriate thoughts—those that don't honor or agree with God—run the show.

ROBERT KOORENNY

These moments of quiet connection are worth the price of admission.

When fear rises, we remind ourselves that God has not given us a spirit of fear (2 Timothy 1:7).

When lust intrudes, we replace it by choosing to focus on what is pure (Philippians 4:8).

When anxiety ambushes us, we pray, rehearse truth, or worship (1 Peter 5:7).

When disappointment whispers, we remind ourselves that God is faithful, in control, and will win in the end (John 16:33).

Each time we align our thoughts with His, we are transformed—or should I say, "We are in the process of transforming"—and positioning to recognize His voice more clearly.

GOD'S THOUGHTS

Scripture and creation both confirm that God's thoughts are not our thoughts, and His ways are not our ways (Isaiah 55:8–9).

Still, He graciously invites us to understand His heart (1 Corinthians 2:10).

I am going to try to frame a few of the areas where God might speak to you or guide you on this journey to truly know His will. This is definitely not a complete list, as He is vast and you are unique.

Here are some topics that He often speaks on:

- **Our relationship with Him** – In the tent, God has reminded me that I have let other things replace Him as my top priority. My time with Him often leads to recalibration. He has also spoken very clearly about His deep love for me and my need for Him. He will do the same for you. He will draw you close and whisper in loving tones when you need it, and at other times, He will point out something that may be eroding your relationship with Jesus.
- **Our character** – My pride has been a topic more than once. He has gently reminded me that I experience the rewards of His blessings

because of His goodness and grace, not because of my exceptional skill and performance. I need Him daily, but sometimes He needs to remind me of this anchoring truth. Each of us has areas where we need to grow. In the tent, God exposes those areas and offers us strength.

- **Our decisions** – God told Abraham to "go to the land I will show you" (Genesis 12:1). If we listen, He will direct us as it pertains to our careers, places we should live, and our relationships. As we lay every decision in front of Him in the tent and then ask for wisdom, He will guide our paths and direct our steps.
- **Our family** – Although our families are always on our prayer lists, sometimes we need to do more than just tell God what we want Him to do for them. We might need to ask Him how we should pray for them or even what wisdom we should share with them. Family dynamics can be tricky. We need to know what to say and when to say it. There are generational gaps, cultural shifts, and even relational struggles, but God knows and is just waiting to impart and assist.

- **Our relationships** – Although we are to be loving and serving to people, there are some relationships that cause harm. They can wear away our convictions, or they can replace priorities. Looking back, relationships seemed to be fraught with more challenges when I was younger—before my family, calling, and character were established—but there are still very real challenges at each step along the way. God is willing and able to help you navigate those relationships while setting expectations and boundaries.
- **Our calling and purpose** – I did not choose youth ministry and evangelism as a career path. God assigned it to me and equipped me for it inside my invisible tent. He spoke to me, encouraged me, and directed me in tangible ways, but He also shaped my passions, perspectives, and paradigms gently over time. Education can play a part, mentorship can help, but there is no substitute for spending time with the Creator who knows why He put you on this earth and what qualities He put inside of you.

- **Our suffering** – Those who have received a horrible diagnosis or who are wrestling with paralyzing grief have found tangible peace and meaningful comfort in His presence. Solitude can amplify pain, but when you invite God into your struggle, it can be a place of great healing.
- **Our daily priorities** – "God, what do you want me to accomplish today?" I have found that this prayer sets my agenda, and it keeps me sane. Rather than try to tackle every important thing in front of me, I watch for the things He will highlight. They hold the biggest priority. Asking God to outline your day ensures you will "run the race" well and accomplish those tasks and responsibilities that are most important.
- **The world around us** – We live in a chaotic world. Full of anger and hate. Full of rumors and conspiracy theories. I love to ask God what He is doing, what is true, and how He wants me to respond to it. Not every need or injustice is a personal assignment. If you ask—and listen—God will point you toward the causes that He wants you to invest your time and treasure in.

JUST FOR YOU

Recently, I found myself struggling.

I'm not sure whether it was pride or jealousy, but I was looking at another ministry with a similar mission to Groundwire, the ministry I founded to help reach young people for Jesus, and I quietly began judging everything about it—the messaging, the strategy, the spending. In my mind, the people leading were doing it wrong and wasting God's money.

If you're thinking, *It was both pride and jealousy,* you're probably right.

After sharing my opinions with a friend (and realizing I had added gossip to the list), I knew I was out of line. So, I pulled out my tent.

I told the Lord what I was thinking. I gave Him my analysis. My conclusions. My opinions. And then I said, "God, I don't like feeling this way. What would You like to say to me?"

I was hoping He would affirm me—that Groundwire was right and the other organization was wrong.

Instead, I heard something like:

"Keep your eyes on your own paper."

And then:

"You can't hold anyone accountable for the vision I've given you."

It was incredibly freeing.

In that moment, I realized I had been trying to play God instead of serving Him. I wanted to manage others instead of remaining faithful to what He had asked of me.

I share this as a caution for all of us.

God does not guide everyone in the same way.

Yes, Scripture gives us absolutes—clear lines of truth and obedience. But most of life is personal. Specific. Sacred ground between God and the individual.

We are responsible to hear God for *ourselves*—not for everyone else.

The tent is not a place to judge, control, or compare. It is a place to be shaped.

We can offer wisdom, but we cannot live someone else's calling. And we cannot hold people accountable for instructions God gave to us.

There is another warning here too:

> *We must enter the tent with humility and honesty.*

Otherwise, we come with our minds already made up—asking God to endorse our conclusions instead of surrendering to His.

When we cling to our own ideas, we build a temple

to our own opinions instead of stepping into a tent of true communion.

Jesus is our friend.
But more than that—He is our Lord.

Our leader.
Our authority.
The One we obey, even when it costs.

It's a difficult lesson.

But if we are always negotiating, always redefining obedience, always pretending we didn't hear Him clearly …

Then we are no longer following Him as Lord.

ASK QUESTIONS

I have found that the people who know me best are the ones who have asked the best (or perhaps the most) questions.

The same is true with God.

He could speak through skywriting, memos (wouldn't that be nice), or even open the mouth of a donkey and call us by name.

However, God is most likely to stick to the patterns that He typically uses. He is most likely to encounter a heart that is turned to Him, someone who has quieted their spirit and is ready to listen. One of the ways we prove that we are ready is by asking questions.

So, ask.

"God, how should I proceed?"
"God, what are You doing in my child's life?"
"God, where should I start today?"

If He whispers, "Call your aunt … ," don't put that off.

If He shares, "You were rude to your coworker and you lost your temper … ," be quick to repent, ask forgiveness of God, ask Him to help you be better, then apologize to your coworker.

At fourteen, I began a simple practice. I would ask God questions—and commit to doing what He said.

I called it "complete obedience."

Often, He gave me a name to pray for. Later, I would discover why.

I once felt directed to pray for a classmate I barely knew and rarely talked to. When I shared with him that I'd prayed for him, he admitted his parents were fighting and he was scared they would divorce.

Another friend told me he had started to read a Christian book, and he was beginning to wonder if God was real. That led to a meaningful Jesus conversation, and I got to pray with him. I learned a couple of years after we graduated that he had given his life to Christ.

Through these stories and many other examples, I learned two things:

God sees perfectly.
And God speaks personally.

Solitude trained me to hear Him.

Because I learned to hear His voice in solitude, my spiritual hearing was trained to hear His voice in the crazy of the day.

Over the years, repetition trained me to recognize Him anywhere.

Even in airports.

God once drew my attention to a wheelchair attendant waiting by my gate. I didn't know her situation, but God's gentle poke led me to start a conversation. I discovered she had just lost her grandmother, and I was able to pray for God's comfort for a sister in Christ.

God is always willing to speak … we just need to learn to listen. Listening for His voice will be something we continue learning all our lives.

I am still learning to let Him interrupt my agenda, replace my conversations, and override my distractions. Sometimes my priorities drift.

But one thing I've seen time and again:

> *There is always a reason behind His whisper, and if we listen, His message is always meaningful.*

NOT ABOUT OUTCOMES

I have learned that everyone prays. Even atheists look up to the sky sometimes and throw up a wish to avoid disaster or for a negative test result to a cancer screening … but most people only pray for outcomes.

They want better jobs, more peace, and happier endings.

This principle of God inviting us to know His will is

not just about influencing outcomes. It is about inviting direction, wisdom, and perspective.

God invites us into something deeper.

To be seen.
To be known.
To truly know.
Real Communion.

We want that and He wants that for us.

When we access the tent to meet with our Jesus, we are accepting His offer to know Him … and to know His will.

This intimate relationship isn't immediate. It takes time to cultivate.

But as we build in this practice, we will truly discover more about who He is and what He desires for us.

Not only does He want us to know His will, but He wants us to see Him clearly.

– 8 –

To See the Righteous One

"The God of our ancestors has chosen you to know His will and to see the Righteous One and to hear words from His mouth" (Acts 22:14).

The invitation to "see the Righteous One" intrigues me. God wants us to see Him as He is—for ourselves—to see Him personally … not through the lens of a preacher, author, parent, or spiritual leader. He wants us to personally discover His beauty and experience His profound presence.

Why?

Because He is better than anything we will ever gaze upon. Greater than any obstacle. Bigger than any problem. More captivating than anything we will ever discover.

And He is more calming, centering, and inspiring than anything else.

One of the promises of the tent is that He, the Righteous One—Jesus—will reveal Himself in deeply personal and meaningful ways.

INSIDE THE TENT

Life can be overwhelming. It can be scary and upsetting.
Every day in the news, you see wars and rumors of wars.

You see pandemics and school shootings.
Bombs going off.
Natural disasters taking lives.
You see anger.
Hatred.
Conflict between people, countries, and ideologies.

You see homelessness, sickness, and disease.
You see poverty, malnutrition, and misery.

All of it takes a toll.
It chips away at your joy.
It discourages you.
It stains your soul.

But when you pitch your tent and climb inside, you come face-to-face with Jesus.

Outside, you deal with darkness and sin.
Inside, you encounter light, hope, and holiness.

When you gaze into His eyes, you look into the eyes of love—perfect love.

The same love that met a woman caught in adultery.
Convinced her she was not condemned but forgiven.
And pointed her toward freedom and a new way of living.

When you experience His presence, you draw near to joy—
Joy that is indescribable and full of glory.

Outside the tent, there is anxiety and depression.
There are moments of happiness, perhaps.
But true joy is rare. But not in the presence of Jesus.

Inside the tent, there is joy.

And there is peace.

Not peace that is fragile.
Not peace that is conditional.

But peace that passes understanding and is bigger than any circumstance.
Peace rooted in the truth that circumstances change, but God does not.

And as you sit with Him, you marinate in a peace that is perfect and does not end.

TOMASZ FILIPEK

But when you
pitch your tent and
climb inside, you
come face-to-face
with Jesus.

As you carve out time with the Creator, you begin to experience:

Love
Joy
Peace
Patience
Kindness
Goodness
Faithfulness
Gentleness
Self-control
(Galatians 5:22–23)

These are not abstract concepts of fruit produced by effort or religious devotion.

These are attributes that define the character and qualities of Jesus.

And when we enter the tent …
When we authentically linger in His presence …

These attributes are what we will see.
What we will hear.
What we will experience.

And ultimately …

They are what we will become.

YOU CAN'T SEE ME

I had a revelation about 2 Corinthians 3:18 a while back—one that helped me understand what God does in us when we spend time in His presence.

The passage begins with Paul describing Moses, so filled with God's glory that his face literally shone. This made the Israelites so uncomfortable that Moses covered himself with a veil to hide the light from them.

Then Paul makes a statement that still applies today:

> *"And we all, who with unveiled faces contemplate the Lord's glory, are being transformed into His image*

with ever-increasing glory, which comes from the Lord, who is the Spirit" (2 Corinthians 3:18).

That realization took me back to high school physics.

I don't remember much about physics, but one concept stuck with me: the law of reflection.

If Mr. Stralser were grading this chapter, I might not get full credit for this definition, but in simple terms, it means this: You don't actually see matter—you see light. You see the light bouncing off the object in front of you.

If you and I were face-to-face, you could reach out and find my hand to shake. You could estimate my height and build. You could describe what I was wearing. But technically, you wouldn't be seeing me. You would be seeing light reflecting off me.

That principle is hidden in this passage.

When we remove the veil—when nothing stands

between us and God's presence—when we climb into the tent, we begin to reflect His glory: His nature, His character, His attributes.

And as we reflect Him, we become like Him.

When we sit with the One who is perfect love, and we let His radiance impact us, we become more loving.

When we dwell with the source of joy, we become more joyful.

When we spend time with the Prince of Peace, peace begins to grow in our hearts.

This is an astonishing truth.

When we "see the Righteous One" and abide with Him, we are not only captivated by His beauty—we are changed by His very nature.

There were seasons in my life when I tried to give myself a pep talk to become better.

I scolded my anger.
I demanded more patience.
I told myself to be more loving and less judgmental.

But I wasn't really changing. I was overcome by those struggles, and I was continually discouraged because of my lack of growth.

However, as I began to spend regular, intentional time in His presence, I started to notice God's movement in my life. I began to recognize change.

Little by little.
Piece by piece.

Not because I convinced myself to be different, but because I was being transformed into His image.

When we accept His invitation to "see the Righteous One," when we invest time in sitting with the One who is perfect in every way and who is everything we long to imitate, we give God access to our souls.

His light begins to reflect—and refract—on us … in us. And He changes us from the inside out.

So, if, like me, there are areas of your life you long to surrender and see changed …

Don't neglect the tent.

If you want harmful habits and toxic attitudes to fade, stop beating yourself up. Stop trying to force change.

Invite Him close.
Enjoy His presence.
And watch the Righteous One shape His masterpiece.

The more time you spend with Him,
the more like Him you will become.

— 9 —

To Hear Words from His Mouth

God's voice does not just *sound* different from the other voices in our lives.

It *is* different.

He never shouts.
He never condescends.
He never manipulates.

When He speaks, He speaks truth and love. He reminds us of His promises.

He encourages.
He drives away insecurity.
He restores hope.

When God speaks to you, you may feel challenges or

experience conviction but never shame.

Even hard truths are wrapped in deep love and unshakable hope.

He points us forward.
He does not trap us in our past.

While others may highlight our weaknesses to discourage or wound us, His voice leaves us strengthened and supported.

For years I've shared the principles of the tent. And along the way, I have started to work in one phrase.

> *When the world points its finger and tells you what you are not, pull out your tent and ask Jesus for a second opinion.*

That phrase carries hope—and a little whimsy.

I don't actually expect people to physically pull out a tent and ask Jesus that question.

ALEXANDER MILO

When the world
points its finger
and tells you what
you are not, pull
out your tent and ask
Jesus for a
second opinion.

But a few have.

And the impact has been unforgettable.

Years ago, while speaking at a youth camp in Indiana, a group of students rushed up to me at breakfast one morning. They had to tell me what happened.

The night before, I had shared these principles and handed out invisible tents. And one young girl decided to use hers.

Some teen boys were trying to impress a group of girls on the basketball court before the day got started. Instead of using manners, they chose cruelty.

One boy pointed at a girl and said, "You are fat. And you are ugly."

He wasn't just careless—he was performing, hoping for approval from his friends and attention from a cute fifteen-year-old nearby.

Most girls would have been crushed.

But the girl who had been insulted remembered what I had said:

> *When the world points its finger and tells you what you are not, pull out your tent and ask Jesus for a second opinion.*

So, she did.

She reached into her back pocket, pulled out her invisible tent, pretended to pop it open, stepped inside, dropped to her knees, and asked—out loud:

> *"Jesus … do You think I'm ugly?"*

Still on her knees, the young girl began to smile.

Then she stood, turned to her attacker, and said, "Jesus says I am not ugly. He says I am the crown of His creation."

The girls around her erupted in cheers.

The boy walked away—awkward and exposed—knowing he had been undone.

You see, the voices of this world are not kind. And they are not reliable.

We need God to remind us that we are valuable. That we are loved.

So, when the voices say otherwise—even the ones inside our own heads—

We must run to Jesus.

Am I worthless?
Am I broken?
Will I ever overcome this sin?

And He will answer—gently and faithfully—

"I am with you.
And you are precious to Me."

MY SHEEP KNOW MY VOICE

Acts 22:14–15 is not the only place where God shows His desire for us to know His voice. We see it again in John 10:2–5:

> *The one who enters by the gate is the shepherd of the sheep. The gatekeeper opens the gate for him, and the sheep listen to his voice. He calls his own sheep by name and leads them out. When he has brought out all his own, he goes on ahead of them, and his sheep follow him because they know his voice. But they will never follow a stranger; in fact, they will run away from him because they do not recognize a stranger's voice.*

Everyone who has placed their trust in Jesus belongs to His family. He is not only our Father—He is our Shepherd.

He provides.
He protects.
He leads.
And yes—He speaks.

This passage beautifully reinforces the heart of this book and the invitation to dwell with Him personally in the tent.

His voice is personal.
Intimacy is implied.

I love that He calls His sheep by name. Our relationship with Him is not generic.

His voice communicates relationship, affection, and identity.

The picture of the sheep and the shepherd speaks of closeness and familiarity. The sheep respond instinctively because they trust him.

There is no fear in their response.

Only recognition.
And safety.

The follower ignores other voices because he knows the voice of the One who loves him and leads him well.

Let's pause there.

That is a real skill—learning to discern between the voice of the Good Shepherd and the many voices competing for our attention.

This passage tells us that discernment can be developed to the point that we don't just hesitate …
We run when we recognize a stranger's voice.

That alone is protection.

Because when you stop following the wrong voices, you stop ending up in dangerous places.

At the root, there are three primary voices competing for your attention:

God.
The enemy.
And your flesh.

Three voices.
Three agendas.
Three very different sounds.

When you learn to quickly recognize who is speaking, you save yourself time, heartache, and regret—and you position yourself to live in a way that pleases the Lord.

So how can you tell the voices apart?

Your flesh always speaks from self-interest.

It does not call you to righteousness.
It does not lead you toward sacrifice.
It speaks with selfish ambition, focused on what benefits you—and only you.

The enemy wants to pull you as far from God as possible.

He doesn't want you obeying God's Word, honoring your commitments, or strengthening your faith.
He speaks through temptation.
He reopens old wounds.
He nudges you toward compromise and disobedience.

God, on the other hand, whispers holiness, servanthood, and discipline.

He speaks of generosity.
Sacrifice.
Conviction.

So, when you're unsure who is speaking, run it through this filter.

Thinking about vulnerably asking a friend if you can pray for them?
The enemy would never suggest that—it draws people toward Jesus.
Your flesh wouldn't either—as it would put you at risk for rejection.

That's likely God.

Considering walking out of a movie because the content has become sexual?
The enemy would want to fuel it—it distracts you away from God.
Your flesh would want you to stay—it feels good and it isn't bothered by temptation.

That's God, protecting your heart.

Feeling drawn to something that is enticing but feeling convicted because it would have to live in secrecy (a relationship, a white lie, slipping out of work early, or taking a little money laying on the counter)?
The enemy would encourage it—whispering "avoid the light, stay in the shadows."
Your flesh would too—living by "pleasure at all costs."

That is God, bringing conviction and drawing you toward holiness.

When you walk closely with the Shepherd, His voice both encourages *and* guards you. God's voice contradicts what your enemy and your flesh have planned for you.

And the more time you spend with Him, the clearer His voice becomes.

Sheep want to stay close.

We simply need to listen—and learn to trust.

HOW?

Some people say, "I want to hear God's voice, but I don't know how."

That's a common concern.

But here's the good news: The ability to hear Him is possible for everyone.

Hearing God's voice is not reserved for spiritual elites.

You don't need an advanced degree.
A high IQ.
Years of service.
Or a head full of memorized Scripture.

The ability to hear God's voice is about closeness.
And training.

It's not just a skill set that you master—it's a relationship.

And like any relationship, there are things you can do to grow in it …
things that will help you hear Him more clearly.

PRACTICE A RHYTHM OF SOLITUDE

I know this may sound redundant, but it matters:

> *When we learn to love the quiet and draw close in a disciplined rhythm, our ability to hear God increases.*

Psalm 84:10 says,

> *"Better is one day in your courts than a thousand elsewhere."*

In the '90s, that verse became a popular worship anthem. I would look around and see hundreds—sometimes thousands—singing that God's presence was their favorite place to be.

But many didn't live that way.

Instead, it was:
"Better is one hour staring at a screen." Or … "Better is one hour on the lake."

I'm not mocking those things. And I'm not saying hobbies are wrong.

But I am saying this:

> *Anyone who truly wants to hear God's voice must prioritize time with Him.*

Sometimes that means saying no to good things so we can say yes to the best thing.

It may mean declining social plans so we can connect with the most important Person in our lives.

Closeness always costs something. You may have to protect your calendar so you have time to do what really matters.

WORSHIP MUSIC CAN BE A TOOL

Psalm 100:4 says that we can enter His gates with thanksgiving and His courts with praise.

This psalm is not just a song that all of us older Christians remember … it is a map and a key.

Gratitude is the first step in crossing the threshold of the tent as we draw near. The pathway into His presence is not complicated; it is carried in a heart that remembers who He is and gives thanks. Each quiet whisper of appreciation for His goodness, His faithfulness, and His unchanging nature gently leads us closer, until we find ourselves standing right next to Him.

Praise then opens the locked chambers of our heart, opening places long closed so we can meet with Jesus without reservation. As we lift our eyes to His endless power and unfailing love, praise becomes more than words—it becomes the key that loosens every chain and releases us from anything that has tried to hold us back.

God-centered, inspirational worship music is one of the best ways to move closer toward Jesus during your tent times.

Worship music is more than melody, rhythm, and harmony.

It sets the table.
It focuses our heart.

Worship music helps redirect our attention—from tasks we need to finish, outcomes we want to control, disappointments we are carrying, or even exciting news we can't shake.

When we pull out our tent and choose to truly connect with God, it doesn't happen instantly.

We have to shift from *go mode* to *abide mode*.

Worship can help us make that transition.

It takes time, but a few songs declaring that God is worthy,
That He is good,
That we trust Him,

They make a remarkable difference.

Yes, my invisible tent comes with a soundtrack.

Perhaps yours will as well.

SCRIPTURE IS ESSENTIAL

Scripture trains our spiritual ears and sharpens our ability to hear.

It leads us and guides us in the ways He has made for us.

> *"Your word is a lamp for my feet, and a light on my path" (Psalm 119:105).*

Because God confirms His voice through His Word—and He never contradicts it—it is vital to include Scripture in your tent time.

People who try to live connected to Christ without investing in His Holy Word will never become fully mature.

> *"All Scripture is God-breathed and is useful for teaching, rebuking, correcting, and training in righteousness, so that the servant of God may be thoroughly equipped for every good work" (2 Timothy 3:16–17).*

CHAPMAN CHOW

There is movement to
God's Word—
it reaches into
vulnerable places.

Often, God uses a passage from His written Word as the starting point for what He wants to say to us. It may be a command, a warning, or the story of someone we can learn from. Or, it could be an image that brings punctuation to something He has been trying to teach us.

God recently amplified a Scripture that I memorized when I was a teenager.

Jude 23 was one that I have known for almost four decades, but God used it to reignite my passion for lost souls. One day while having a conversation in my tent about my heart for the lost, I told Him I wanted my burden to grow. I didn't want to "act" out of duty or serve so others would be impressed. I said, "God, remind me of what truly awaits those who do not know you as their personal Lord and Savior."

A few minutes later, I ended up at "save others by snatching them from the fire" (Jude 23).

Immediately, the imagery of that verse grabbed me.

I knew that misery awaited those who die without knowing Jesus. That truth restoked my fire for those who are lost and has stayed with me ever since.

As Scripture reminds us:

> *"For the word of God is alive and active. Sharper than any double-edged sword … it judges the thoughts and attitudes of the heart" (Hebrews 4:12).*

There is movement to God's Word—it reaches into vulnerable places.
It is active, not passive; it engages, confronts, and changes us.
It discerns what honors God and what does not.
Then it trims away attitudes, behaviors, and vices that don't belong.

His Word is powerful, faithful, and piercing.
Convicting, commanding, authoritative.

Yet, it is also irresistible, cleansing, and healing.

You will not only read His Word—His Word will
read you.
You will not only learn what He says—you will be
transformed by what He says.

Make the Bible central to your quiet time with the Lord.

And don't just read Scripture—memorize it.

The deeper God's Word settles into your heart, mind, and soul, the more clearly you will recognize the voice of its Author.

COMMIT TO THE NUDGE

The tent is not about passively learning to listen, linger, and live in God's presence only. It is also about allowing Him to use you to bring hope, joy, and impact to those around you.

I call active listening (when we are ready to obey His direction) "committing to the nudge."

The tent is where you learn to listen for the nudge, and the more you respond to it, the more He knows He can trust you with it.

In chapter 7, we talked about complete obedience—the simple, interactive "game" I created to help me learn to recognize God's voice.

Let me remind you of the pattern:

Ask questions.
Invite His voice.
And commit to the nudge.

Recently, a friend told me he has decided to follow through whenever he senses something *might* be from God—even when it doesn't make sense.

One day, while searching his phone for a different number, his aunt's name appeared. He hadn't spoken to her in months, but he felt prompted to reach out.

So, he texted, *Hi, I was just thinking about you.*

Immediately, his phone rang.

It was his aunt—crying.

"Thank you for remembering my birthday," she said. "I thought everyone had forgotten."

He didn't tell her the truth—that he had forgotten. He simply told her that he loved her, that he was praying for her, and that he was grateful for her.

A simple nudge.
A real need.
A divine connection.

God often works that way.

Recently, my wife, Jené, and I were at a ministry event when God nudged her.

While talking with a woman, Jené sensed something was wrong and gently asked, "Are you okay? I feel like you might be carrying something heavy."

The woman immediately shared about a difficult situation her family was facing. Tears came as Jené prayed for her.

Later, the woman said how grateful she was—how seen and known she felt.

That's what obedience does.

So often, God uses our simple yes to encourage hearts and meet real needs.

GOD WANTS TO SPEAK TO YOU.

It may be hard to believe, but God truly wants to speak to you.

He wants you to know what He is thinking. And He wants to silence every voice—internal and external—that has ever lied to you.

If you listen, He will remind you:

You bring Him pleasure.
He will never leave you.
He has your back.

Sometimes His voice is very specific:

Don't take that job.
Go back to school.
Pray for your son.

If we aren't hearing Him regularly, it may be because we haven't made the time … or we haven't learned how.

But we can make the time.
And with time, we can learn.

Often, it begins by stopping our talking long enough to listen—because God rarely interrupts.

As His sheep, we long to hear His voice.

What's remarkable is that He wants to speak to us even more than we want to hear Him.

And when we do listen, He speaks.

And when He speaks, the rewards are rich:

Direction.
Comfort.
Peace.
Guidance.
Life.
Protection.
Purpose.

So now is the time to accept the invitation.

It's time to:

lean in,
listen closely,
trust deeply,

And follow boldly.

— 10 —

Then . . . You Will Be His Witness

So many people want to make a difference. They want to have an impact on the world. They want to spread hope and love. They want to share joy and peace. Many Christians want to share Jesus. But they might not know how.

They get the process confused.

They approach things in the wrong order.

They are focused on trying to make a difference when Scripture teaches them to focus on Jesus first.

They are trying to bypass the process that God uses to build history makers.

ONE LITTLE POST-IT NOTE

One day, during some extended tent time with the Lord, I told Him about the impact I longed to have.

For as long as I can remember, I've wanted God to use me to bring light to those in darkness and to share Jesus with the lost and broken. I've prayed that prayer for decades.

At first, those prayers carried more pride than purity. I wanted significance. Recognition. To be seen as effective.

But over time, God changed my heart.

Now my desire is simple: that more people would know His love and forgiveness.

I'm convinced that those who live under the lordship of Jesus experience deeper joy and fewer regrets. And more importantly, I know that only through Him can they find eternal life.

SAMANTHA OAKEY

God, build me in private so You can use me in public.

So I still pray, "God, let me share Your love"—but not so I can be noticed. Only so Jesus will be known.

As I shared this with Him in my tent time that day, God gently reminded me that this desire began with Him.

He longs for people to come to the truth and be saved (1 Timothy 2:3–4). And He is willing to use ordinary people—like me—to spread the gospel.

Then He showed me the process He uses to shape world-changers.

He whispered:

"I build people in private so I can use them in public."

I grabbed a yellow Post-it and wrote:

God, build me in private so You can use me in public.

That sentence has challenged me ever since.

Like many, I want God to use me publicly. It is very likely that you want God to work through you as well.

But to accomplish His plans for us, for Him to use us, we cannot bypass the process.

We must invest in time alone in the tent.

To learn His voice. Listen to it.
Abide in His presence. Linger.

Because it is there—away from the spotlight—that He molds us, shapes us, and transforms us …

To look like Him,
To think like Him,
To care about what He cares about,
And to respond when He moves.

God builds us in private so He can use us in public.

That is true for each one of us.

And it was true for Paul.

AFTER THE TENT

Revisiting Acts 22:14, Ananias tells Saul that God has chosen him to know His will, to see the Righteous One, and to hear His voice—to live in a rhythm of knowing God personally.

That alone would be enough for a fulfilled life.

The Creator calling us close.
Inviting us into intimacy.

But verse 15 adds even more perspective.

One of the fruits of that closeness is this:

> *"You will be His witness to all people of what you have seen and heard."*

God was preparing Saul to share truth.
To carry perspective.

He was shaping him as a leader.
He was building him into a representative.

We know from Galatians 1:16–18 that Paul withdrew from the public eye for as long as three years. Scripture does not detail how he structured those three years, but we can be confident that God was forming him in private as He was preparing to use him in public—shaping the man who would leave a legacy of lasting impact.

And He does the same with us.

WHEN WE WALK OUT

Although God's presence and His Spirit always go with us, there are times when we must leave the tent.

We go to work.
We chauffeur kids.
We serve at church.

It's not that He leaves us—or stops whispering.

It's that the *undivided focus* we enjoy in the tent is no longer convenient.

When we step outside the invisible tent, we carry with us what we have seen and heard.

And God opens doors for us to share it.

Perhaps you are talking with a coworker and sense their loneliness—their feelings of being unseen and unloved.

But you have just been with perfect love, and you carry that with you everywhere you go. You have experienced a love that is unconditional and unending—and you know it is not only for you but for them … for everyone.

So, you say,

"I want you to know that you are loved. And God has never left you." And you begin a conversation where you are able to encourage and pray with your friend.

Why?

Because you just experienced pure love from the Righteous One in the tent.

Perhaps you follow someone on social media who is desperate.
They need a miracle—health, finances, hope.

Something rises up in you.

You have just been in the tent with the
miracle-working God.

Your faith is strong.
You know He is able.

So, instead of keeping it to yourself, you reach out and offer to pray.

Not an "I'll pray for you" out of pity kind of
prayer …

But a:

"My God can meet this need.
He can move that mountain.
He can kick down that door" kind of prayer.

You saw it, you heard it, you were close to it, and you were able to be a witness to it.

Because everything you experience in the tent changes you.

And it also shapes you into the most powerful witness you can be.

You are no longer speaking only of Bible stories.

No longer repeating theory.

You know the Author of Creation and the Giver of Life.

You are intimately connected to the One who loves perfectly and forgives without limit.

You know His will.
You have gazed on His beauty.
You have heard His voice.

And now you can speak of Him boldly.

We must learn that the most effective people at praying for others, sharing hope, and leading others to Jesus are not those with the most impressive degrees or polished skills …

They are those who have been shaped in His presence. Those who are willing to be His witnesses of what they have seen and heard.

So, don't try to change the world until you have let Him change you.

Don't try to seize the day until you have spent time with the King.

Draw near.
Listen well.
Receive His peace.

And when you leave the tent? Be ready.

He is going to use you in remarkable and
God-honoring ways.

THE END OF THE BOOK ...
BUT THE BEGINNING OF THE JOURNEY

So, we have come to this moment. It is time for the book to end.

I have done my best to show you that God is eagerly waiting for you to accept His invitation—to step into the tent.

He wants to reveal Himself to you.

He wants to change you.

Remember that the principles of the tent are true:

> *Anyone can go in.*
> *God's presence will show up.*

Intimate communication will take place.
And you can stay as long as you want.

When you pitch the tent, He is already waiting.

He has chosen you—

To know Him,
To know His will,
To see the Righteous One,
And to hear His voice.

And then …

You will become a witness
To what you have seen and heard.

The secrets of the invisible tent changed my life.

And I believe they can change yours too.

About the Author

Sean Dunn is the Founder and CEO of Groundwire Ministries and author of *Contending for the Rising Generations*. He has introduced thousands to God's invitation to meet with Him, walk with Him, and be transformed by Him. Sean and his wife, Jené, live in Colorado, where they pursue a daily rhythm of intimacy with God.

Secrets of the Tent

A Field Guide

The invitation to know God personally has already been given—not by an author or by a preacher, but by the Creator Himself. He longs for you to draw near, to know Him, to trust Him, and to be transformed by Him.

The Invisible Tent is a picture of what God is offering—and how to experience it in a personal and powerful way.

Inside this tent:

Anyone can go in.
God's presence will show up.
Intimate communication will take place.
You can stay as long as you want.

A PRAYER TO PRAY

God, thank You for inviting me into Your presence. Thank You for drawing near to me every time I draw near to You. Thank You for speaking to me face-to-face, as one speaks to a friend, and for allowing me to linger with You.

Help me become addicted to Your presence. Help me receive everything You desire to give me in our quiet times together. Meet me, change me, and send me.

In the precious name of Jesus,

Amen.

God is waiting to meet you in the tent—
in a real and meaningful way.
He desires to reveal Himself to you.
And if you receive all that He longs to give,
you will never be the same.

The God of our fathers has chosen you:

To know Him—
deeply, personally, powerfully

To know His will

To see the Righteous One

To hear the words from His mouth

Then

To be a witness of what you have
both seen and heard

A PRAYER TO PRAY

God, thank You for choosing me to know You. Teach me Your will. Help me to see You as You truly are, and to discern Your voice clearly.

Teach me to enjoy Your presence, to linger with You, and to be changed by You. Help me shut out every other noise so I can recognize You more fully.

And Lord, I commit that I will not keep to myself what You show me, teach me, and speak to me in the tent. I will be a witness to what I have seen and heard.

Thank You for inviting me close. I am grateful—and eager—for this journey.

In the mighty name of Jesus,

Amen.

Made in the USA
Coppell, TX
27 June 2026

83631357R20114